VIRGINIA TEST PREP

Practice Test Book

SOL Math

Grade 3

ISBN 978-1482727494

CONTENTS

INTRODUCTION
For Parents, Teachers, and Tutors

About the Book

This practice test book contains three complete SOL Mathematics tests. The tests are just like the tests given by the state. Each test contains the same question types and styles, tests the same skills, and has the same length as the state test. If students can master the tests in this book, they will be prepared and ready to master the real SOL Mathematics test.

Taking the Test

Each test contains multiple-choice questions and questions that mimic the new technology-enhanced questions used on the state test. Students should answer the multiple-choice questions by filling in the circle of their answer choice in the test book. For the technology-enhanced questions, students should follow the instructions given with the question.

Timing the Test

Just like the real SOL Mathematics test, each practice test is divided into two sections. When taking the real SOL Mathematics test, students may complete both sections on the same day, or may complete each section on two consecutive days. If both sections are completed on the same day, students are given a break of at least 15 minutes between the two sections.

Students are given as much time as they need, but are expected to complete each section in about 60 minutes. It is not essential to time the test, but it is good preparation to ensure that students can complete each section in about 60 minutes.

Use of Calculators

Students are not allowed to use a calculator when taking the real SOL Mathematics test. Students should complete the practice tests without the use of a calculator.

TECHNOLOGY-ENHANCED QUESTIONS
For Parents, Teachers, and Tutors

The real SOL Mathematics test will include four types of technology-enhanced questions. These types are described below.

Fill-in-the-Blank Questions

Students type in letters, numbers, or symbols. These questions usually contain a blank box for students to type their answers into.

Drag and Drop Questions

Students move one or more draggers to drop zones on the screen. Draggers could be words, numbers, shapes, equations, or other elements. For examples, students may be asked to place all the rectangles in one drop zone, or may be asked to drag numbers to place them in order from lowest to highest.

Hot Spot Questions

Students select one or more hot spot zones. These hot spot zones are usually part of a chart, graph, or illustration. For example, students may select a point on a number line, a point on a coordinate plane, or a point on a shape. Students may also be asked to answer fraction questions by selecting shapes or parts of a shape to shade them.

Bar Graph or Histogram

Students complete a bar graph or histogram by creating a bar or column with the correct height or length.

This practice test book contains questions with similar formats to the technology-enhanced questions. They mimic the same processes that students will use to answer these questions online. These questions will help students become familiar with the formats of the technology-enhanced questions.

SOL MATHEMATICS

GRADE 3

PRACTICE TEST 1

SECTION 1

Instructions

Read each question carefully. For each multiple-choice question, fill in the circle for the correct answer. For other types of questions, follow the instructions given.

1 There are 1,920 students at Jenna's school. Which of these is another way to write 1,920?

  Ⓐ   1,000 + 900 + 20

  Ⓑ   1,000 + 900 + 2

  Ⓒ   1,000 + 90 + 20

  Ⓓ   1,000 + 90 + 2

2 The graph shows the number of points four players scored in a basketball game.

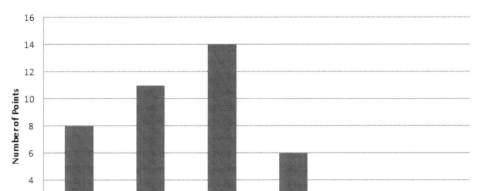

Fran scored 9 points and Emiko scored 5 points. Add two bars to the graph to show the points scored by Fran and Emiko.

3   What do the shaded models below show?

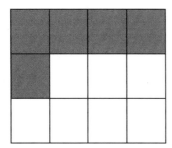 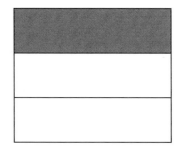

Ⓐ $\dfrac{5}{12} > \dfrac{1}{3}$

Ⓑ $\dfrac{5}{12} = \dfrac{1}{3}$

Ⓒ $\dfrac{5}{12} < \dfrac{4}{12}$

Ⓓ $\dfrac{5}{7} < \dfrac{2}{3}$

4   Leah made 500 cakes of soap to sell at a fair. She sold 182 cakes of soap on Saturday. Then she sold 218 cakes of soap on Sunday. Which expression could be used to find how many cakes of soap Leah had left over?

Ⓐ   500 + 182 + 218

Ⓑ   500 + 182 − 218

Ⓒ   500 − 182 + 218

Ⓓ   500 − 182 − 218

5 Michael drove 1,285 miles during a vacation. Which digit is in the tens place in the number 1,285?

Ⓐ 1

Ⓑ 2

Ⓒ 8

Ⓓ 5

6 Donna has 18 roses. She wants to put the roses into vases so that each vase has the same number of roses, with no roses left over.

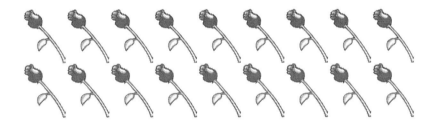

How many roses could Donna put in each vase?

Ⓐ 4

Ⓑ 5

Ⓒ 6

Ⓓ 8

7   Shade the stars below so that $\frac{5}{9}$ of the stars are shaded.

8   Patrick bought 2 packets of 8 pencils for $4 per packet. He also bought 3 packets of 5 crayons for $3 per packet. How much did Patrick spend in all?

Ⓐ $17

Ⓑ $25

Ⓒ $47

Ⓓ $64

9   Look at the shaded figure below.

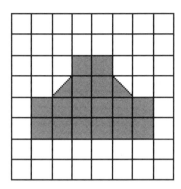

What is the area of the shaded figure?

Ⓐ   17 square units

Ⓑ   16 square units

Ⓒ   18 square units

Ⓓ   24 square units

10   Billy collects pennies and nickels. Billy has 142 pennies and 56 nickels in his coin collection. Which is the best estimate of the total number of coins in Billy's collection?

Ⓐ   150

Ⓑ   180

Ⓒ   200

Ⓓ   250

11   Circle all the shapes below that are quadrilaterals.

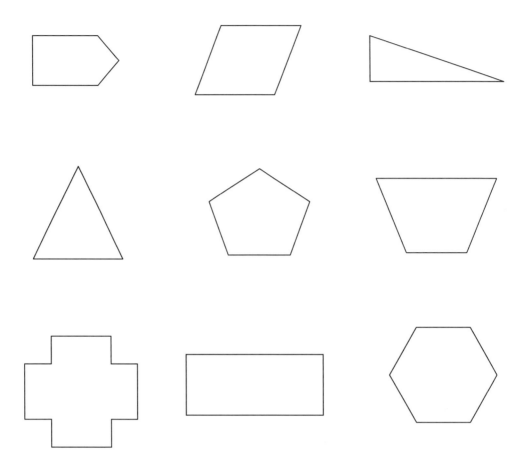

12 The figure below models the number sentence 6 × 2 = 12.

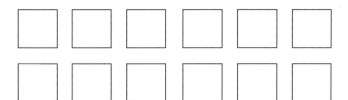

Which number sentence is modeled by the same figure?

Ⓐ   6 ÷ 2 = 3

Ⓑ   36 ÷ 3 = 12

Ⓒ   12 ÷ 6 = 2

Ⓓ   24 ÷ 2 = 12

13 Which number makes the number sentence below true? Write the number in the box.

$$18 \times \boxed{} = 18$$

14   Look at the triangle below.

Which of the following shapes appears to be congruent to the triangle above?

Ⓐ

Ⓑ

Ⓒ

Ⓓ

15 Which measurement is the best estimate of the length of a swimming pool?

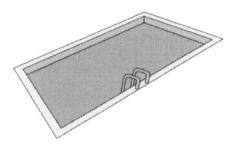

   Ⓐ   10 millimeters

   Ⓑ   10 centimeters

   Ⓒ   10 kilometers

   Ⓓ   10 meters

16 Kira was asked to make a number using only the digits 1, 5, 8, and 9. She could only use each digit once. What is the largest number Kira could make? Write your answer on the lines below.

_____, _____ _____ _____

17 A school play was performed on three nights. The table below shows the number of people that saw the school play each night.

Day	Number of People
Friday	225
Saturday	342
Sunday	290

Which number sentence shows the best estimate of the total number of people who saw the school play?

Ⓐ   200 + 300 + 200 = 700

Ⓑ   200 + 300 + 300 = 800

Ⓒ   200 + 400 + 300 = 900

Ⓓ   300 + 400 + 300 = 1,000

18   Aaron has quarters and dimes. Aaron's coins are shown below.

What fraction of the coins are quarters?

Ⓐ $\frac{1}{2}$

Ⓑ $\frac{1}{3}$

Ⓒ $\frac{2}{3}$

Ⓓ $\frac{3}{5}$

19 Which number sentence represents the array shown below?

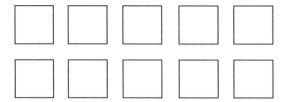

Ⓐ   5 + 2 = 7

Ⓑ   5 × 5 = 25

Ⓒ   5 × 2 = 10

Ⓓ   5 − 2 = 3

20 Which point on the number line represents $2\frac{3}{4}$?

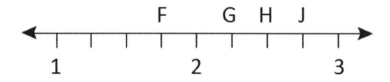

Ⓐ   Point F

Ⓑ   Point G

Ⓒ   Point H

Ⓓ   Point J

21 The table below shows the different colors of marbles in a bag.

Color	Number of Marbles
Red	5
Green	10
Blue	2
White	3

If Mike selects 1 marble at random, which color will he most likely select?

Ⓐ   Red

Ⓑ   Green

Ⓒ   Blue

Ⓓ   White

22   Leah baked 3 pies. She cut each pie into 8 pieces.

How many pieces of pie does Leah have?

Ⓐ   24

Ⓑ   16

Ⓒ   18

Ⓓ   32

23   Which shape has more sides than a pentagon?

Ⓐ   Triangle

Ⓑ   Square

Ⓒ   Hexagon

Ⓓ   Rectangle

24 A dollar bill has a length of about 150 mm and a width of about 50 mm.

Which is the best estimate of the perimeter of a dollar bill?

Ⓐ   200 mm

Ⓑ   300 mm

Ⓒ   400 mm

Ⓓ   600 mm

25 Which shape is **NOT** part of the solid object below?

Ⓐ   Cone

Ⓑ   Cube

Ⓒ   Cylinder

Ⓓ   Hemisphere

END OF SECTION 1

SOL MATHEMATICS

GRADE 3

PRACTICE TEST 1

SECTION 2

Instructions

Read each question carefully. For each multiple-choice question, fill in the circle for the correct answer. For other types of questions, follow the instructions given.

26 Troy swapped 2 quarters for coins with the same value. Which of these could Troy have swapped his 2 quarters for?

Ⓐ   25 pennies

Ⓑ   20 nickels

Ⓒ   10 nickels

Ⓓ   10 dimes

27 Andrew is selling muffins at a bake sale. The table shows the profit he makes by selling 5, 10, 15, and 20 muffins.

Muffins Sold	Profit Made
5	$15
10	$30
15	$45
20	$60

Based on the table above, how much profit does Andrew make for selling 1 muffin?

Ⓐ $15

Ⓑ $5

Ⓒ $3

Ⓓ $2

28 Kai found the coins shown below in the sofa. What is the value of the coins that Kai found?

   Ⓐ $1.26

   Ⓑ $1.36

   Ⓒ $1.45

   Ⓓ $2.36

29   Mario buys screws in packets of 6.

If Mario counts the screws in groups of 6, which of these numbers would he count? Circle all the numbers that he would count.

16   18   22

30   36   40

30   Mrs. Bowen cooked dinner for 24 guests. She cooked 3 courses for each guest. Which equation shows how many courses Mrs. Bowen cooked?

Ⓐ $24 \times 3 = 72$

Ⓑ $24 + 3 = 27$

Ⓒ $24 - 3 = 21$

Ⓓ $24 \div 3 = 8$

31   Which number is 3 more than the product of 4 and 23?

   Ⓐ   80

   Ⓑ   89

   Ⓒ   92

   Ⓓ   95

32   The graph below shows the high temperature in Dallas, Texas for five days.

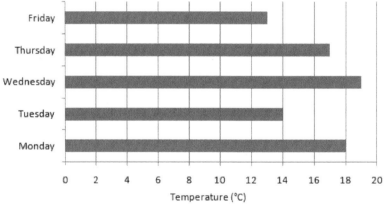

On which day was the high temperature 17°C?

   Ⓐ   Tuesday

   Ⓑ   Wednesday

   Ⓒ   Thursday

   Ⓓ   Friday

33 Which model is shaded to show a fraction equivalent to $\frac{6}{8}$?

Ⓐ

Ⓑ

Ⓒ

Ⓓ

34 Beads are sold in packets of 6 or packets of 8. Liz needs to buy exactly 30 beads. Which set of packets could Liz buy?

Ⓐ   1 packet of 8 beads and 2 packets of 6 beads

Ⓑ   2 packets of 8 beads and 2 packets of 6 beads

Ⓒ   1 packet of 8 beads and 3 packets of 6 beads

Ⓓ   3 packets of 8 beads and 1 packet of 6 beads

35 Joy had $18. She bought a pair of shorts for $11. Then she bought a scarf for $3. Which expression shows one way to find how much money Joy had left?

Ⓐ   18 + 11 + 3

Ⓑ   18 + 11 − 3

Ⓒ   18 − 11 + 3

Ⓓ   18 − 11 − 3

36 Chan started the number pattern below.

4, 8, 12, 16, 20, ____, ____

If Chan continues the number pattern, which two numbers will come next?

Ⓐ   22, 24

Ⓑ   24, 28

Ⓒ   28, 36

Ⓓ   40, 80

37 The graph below shows how long Jody studied each week day.

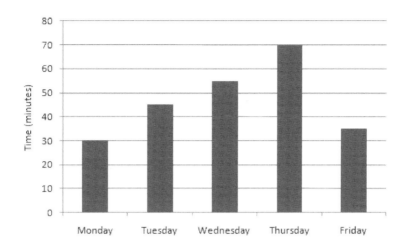

On which day did Jody study for between 40 and 50 minutes?

Ⓐ   Tuesday

Ⓑ   Wednesday

Ⓒ   Thursday

Ⓓ   Friday

38 Reggie's train leaves at the time shown on the clock below.

What time does Reggie's train leave?

Ⓐ   3:00

Ⓑ   1:15

Ⓒ   1:10

Ⓓ   3:05

39 Davis is making a pictograph to show how many letters three students wrote in a month.

Davis	✉✉✉
Bobby	
Inga	✉✉

Each ✉ means 2 letters.

Bobby wrote 8 letters. How many letter symbols should Davis use to show 8 letters?

Ⓐ 8

Ⓑ 4

Ⓒ 2

Ⓓ 16

40 Bindu is slicing apples into 8 slices. Which table shows how many apple slices Bindu will have if she uses 2, 4, and 5 apples?

Ⓐ

Number of Apples	Number of Slices
2	16
4	32
5	40

Ⓑ

Number of Apples	Number of Slices
2	8
4	32
5	40

Ⓒ

Number of Apples	Number of Slices
2	8
4	32
5	20

Ⓓ

Number of Apples	Number of Slices
2	10
4	20
5	25

41 The graph below shows how long Jason studied for one week.

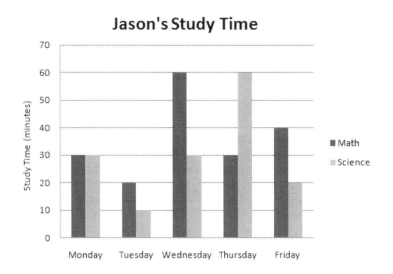

How long did Jason study science for on Thursday?

Ⓐ   30 minutes

Ⓑ   60 minutes

Ⓒ   90 minutes

Ⓓ   20 minutes

42   Look at the figure below.

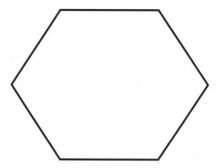

How many edges and vertices does the figure have? Write your answer on the lines below.

Edges: _____

Vertices: _____

43 Which word best describes the shape of each layer of the wedding cake?

   Ⓐ   Cone

   Ⓑ   Cube

   Ⓒ   Cylinder

   Ⓓ   Sphere

44 Which fraction does the shaded model represent?

 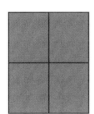 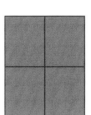  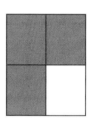

   Ⓐ $4\frac{3}{4}$

   Ⓑ $4\frac{1}{4}$

   Ⓒ $5\frac{3}{4}$

   Ⓓ $5\frac{1}{4}$

45 Josephine boarded a train at 10:40 a.m. She got off the train at 11:35 a.m. How long was she on the train for?

    Ⓐ   45 minutes

    Ⓑ   55 minutes

    Ⓒ   65 minutes

    Ⓓ   95 minutes

46 Carmen tossed a coin 10 times. The coin landed on heads 6 times and tails 4 times. She wants to complete the tally chart below to show the results.

Heads	Tails

Which of these should Carmen place in the "Heads" column?

    Ⓐ ||||

    Ⓑ   卌

    Ⓒ   卌 |

    Ⓓ   卌 ||

47 Which fraction model is equivalent to $\frac{1}{2}$?

Ⓐ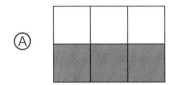

Ⓑ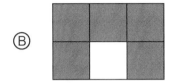

Ⓒ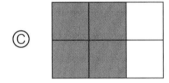

Ⓓ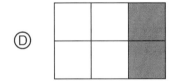

48 Sally is making a pictograph to show how many students are in grade 3, grade 4, and grade 5.

Grade 3	☺☺☺☺☺☺☺☺☺☺☺
Grade 4	☺☺☺☺☺☺☺☺☺☺☺☺☺
Grade 5	

☺ = 5 students

There are 65 students in grade 5. Which of these should Sally use to represent 65 students?

Ⓐ ☺☺☺☺☺☺☺☺☺☺☺

Ⓑ ☺☺☺☺☺☺☺☺☺☺☺☺

Ⓒ ☺☺☺☺☺☺☺☺☺☺☺☺☺

Ⓓ ☺☺☺☺☺☺☺☺☺☺☺☺☺☺

49 Kai drove for 4 hours. How many minutes did Kyle drive for?

     Ⓐ   180 minutes

     Ⓑ   240 minutes

     Ⓒ   320 minutes

     Ⓓ   400 minutes

50 What fraction of the model is shaded?

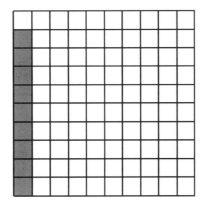

     Ⓐ $\dfrac{1}{9}$

     Ⓑ $\dfrac{9}{10}$

     Ⓒ $\dfrac{9}{91}$

     Ⓓ $\dfrac{9}{100}$

END OF SECTION 2

SOL MATHEMATICS

GRADE 3

PRACTICE TEST 2

SECTION 1

Instructions

Read each question carefully. For each multiple-choice question, fill in the circle for the correct answer. For other types of questions, follow the instructions given.

1 There are 30,804 people living in Montville. Which of these is another way to write 30,804?

Ⓐ 30,000 + 800 + 4

Ⓑ 30 + 80 + 4

Ⓒ 3,000 + 800 + 40

Ⓓ 300 + 80 + 4

2 The graph below shows the number of pets four girls have.

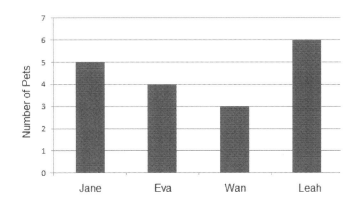

Which two girls have 10 pets in total?

Ⓐ Jane and Eva

Ⓑ Wan and Leah

Ⓒ Eva and Leah

Ⓓ Leah and Wan

3   Plot the number 48 on the number line below.

4   Rory scored 28 points in a basketball game. Adam scored 4 points less than Rory. Danny scored 6 points more than Adam. How many points did Danny score?

Ⓐ   18

Ⓑ   30

Ⓒ   26

Ⓓ   38

5 There were 17,856 people living in Eastwood in 2009. What is the value of the digit 8 in 17,856?

Ⓐ Eight hundred

Ⓑ Eight thousand

Ⓒ Eighty thousand

Ⓓ Eighty

6 Chan had a bag of 28 lollipops. He divided the lollipops evenly between several children.

If there were no lollipops left over, how many lollipops could each child have received?

Ⓐ 6

Ⓑ 7

Ⓒ 8

Ⓓ 9

7   Which picture shows that $\frac{2}{5}$ of the shapes are hearts?

Ⓐ

Ⓑ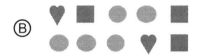

Ⓒ

Ⓓ

8   Ally bought 3 packets of pencils and 2 packets of pens. There were 8 pencils in each packet, and 6 pens in each packet. Which expression could be used to find how many more pencils she bought than pens?

Ⓐ $(8 \times 6) - (3 \times 2)$

Ⓑ $(8 - 3) \times (6 - 2)$

Ⓒ $(3 \times 8) - (2 \times 6)$

Ⓓ $(3 + 8) - (2 + 6)$

9   Georgia made the design below.

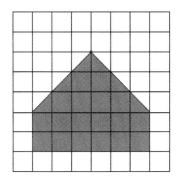

Each square on the grid measures 1 square centimeter. What is the area of the shaded part of the design?

Ⓐ   21 square centimeters

Ⓑ   24 square centimeters

Ⓒ   18 square centimeters

Ⓓ   20 square centimeters

10   Ling scored 82 on a reading test. Mickey scored 63 on the reading test. Which is the best estimate of how many more points Ling scored than Mickey?

Ⓐ   10

Ⓑ   15

Ⓒ   20

Ⓓ   25

11 Mr. Porter is choosing dance partners for the girls in his class. He places the names of the boys in a hat. He then has each girl select a name from the hat.

Roland	Ewan	Davis
Greg	Colin	Archer

Emily selects first. What is the probability that Emily selects Colin?

Ⓐ   1 out of 5

Ⓑ   4 out of 5

Ⓒ   1 out of 6

Ⓓ   5 out of 6

12 A diner has 18 tables. Each table can seat 4 people. The diner also has 8 benches that can each seat 6 people. How many people can the diner seat in all?

Ⓐ   36

Ⓑ   120

Ⓒ   260

Ⓓ   308

13   Which shape has fewer sides than a pentagon?

    Ⓐ   Heptagon

    Ⓑ   Square

    Ⓒ   Hexagon

    Ⓓ   Octagon

14   Look at the triangle below.

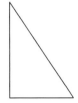

Circle all the shapes that appear to be congruent to the triangle.

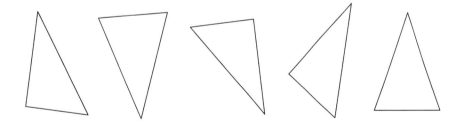

15 Which measurement is the most likely length of a crayon?

Ⓐ   4 feet

Ⓑ   4 inches

Ⓒ   4 yards

Ⓓ   4 miles

16 The grade 3 students at Sam's school are collecting cans for a food drive. The table below shows how many cans each class collected.

Class	Number of Cans
Miss Powell	39
Mr. Sato	42
Mrs. Joshi	26
Mr. Perez	37

Which number sentence shows the best estimate of the total number of cans collected?

Ⓐ   40 + 40 + 30 + 40 = 150

Ⓑ   40 + 40 + 20 + 40 = 140

Ⓒ   40 + 40 + 20 + 30 = 130

Ⓓ   30 + 40 + 20 + 30 = 120

17   On Monday, there were 21 students in a dance class. There were 4 students missing from the class. How many students are usually in the dance class?

(A)   25

(B)   21

(C)   17

(D)   19

18   Janine bought a packet of muffins. The packet contained 4 chocolate muffins and 6 vanilla muffins.

What fraction of the muffins were vanilla?

(A) $\frac{1}{2}$

(B) $\frac{1}{3}$

(C) $\frac{2}{3}$

(D) $\frac{3}{5}$

19   The table below shows the colors of blocks in a bag.

Color	Number of Blocks
Red	6
Green	4
Blue	7
White	2

If Andre picks one block at random, which color will he be least likely to pick?

Ⓐ   Red

Ⓑ   Green

Ⓒ   Blue

Ⓓ   White

20   What fraction does point *J* represent?

Ⓐ $2\frac{1}{4}$

Ⓑ $2\frac{1}{3}$

Ⓒ $2\frac{1}{5}$

Ⓓ $2\frac{1}{2}$

21 Which two shapes is the object below made up of? Circle the two shapes.

cone   sphere   triangular prism

cube   cylinder   rectangular prism

22 A pizza has 8 slices.

Eriko wants to order enough pizza to have at least 62 slices. What is the least number of pizzas Eriko could order?

Ⓐ 7

Ⓑ 8

Ⓒ 9

Ⓓ 10

23   Tina completes the calculation below.

$$8 \times 5 = 40$$

Which of the following could Tina use to check her calculation?

Ⓐ $40 \div 5 = 8$

Ⓑ $8 \times 8 = 64$

Ⓒ $40 + 5 = 45$

Ⓓ $5 \times 40 = 200$

24   Which measurement is the most likely length of a briefcase?

Ⓐ   30 millimeters

Ⓑ   30 centimeters

Ⓒ   30 kilometers

Ⓓ   30 meters

25 Habib measured the length of each wall of his room. A diagram of Habib's room is shown below.

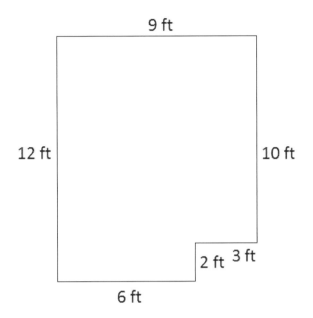

What is the perimeter of Habib's room?

Ⓐ   37 ft

Ⓑ   40 ft

Ⓒ   39 ft

Ⓓ   42 ft

END OF SECTION 1

SOL MATHEMATICS

GRADE 3

PRACTICE TEST 2

SECTION 2

Instructions

Read each question carefully. For each multiple-choice question, fill in the circle for the correct answer. For other types of questions, follow the instructions given.

26 Lee wrote the set of expressions below.

$$5 + 5 \qquad 5 \times 2 \qquad 3 + 7 \qquad 12 - 2$$

Which expression could be added to the set?

Ⓐ $6 + 4$

Ⓑ $10 + 2$

Ⓒ 5×3

Ⓓ $8 - 1$

27 Apples are sold in bags. There are the same number of apples in each bag. The table below shows the number of apples in 2, 3, and 4 bags.

Number of Bags	Number of Apples
2	12
3	18
4	24
6	

Based on the table above, how many apples are in 6 bags?

Ⓐ   30

Ⓑ   28

Ⓒ   36

Ⓓ   42

28 Mia bought a milkshake. She was given the change shown below. How much change was Mia given?

Ⓐ $0.76

Ⓑ $0.71

Ⓒ $0.51

Ⓓ $0.66

29   Toni has tokens for arcade games.

If Toni counts her tokens in groups of 6, which list shows only numbers she would count?

Ⓐ   6, 8, 10, 12

Ⓑ   6, 10, 16, 20

Ⓒ   12, 18, 24, 30

Ⓓ   12, 16, 20, 24

30   Damon is 51 inches tall. Alka is 57 inches tall. Gemma is 49 inches tall. Write the numbers given in the spaces below to correctly compare the heights.

_____ inches < _____ inches < _____ inches

31 Which number is greater than 5,167?

Ⓐ 5,096

Ⓑ 5,203

Ⓒ 5,159

Ⓓ 5,164

32 The table below shows Emma's savings over four months.

Month	Amount Saved ($)
Jan	19
Feb	16
Mar	14
Apr	18

Complete the graph below using the data in the table.

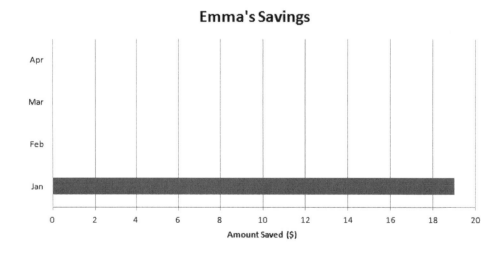

33 Look at the group of numbers below. Circle all the numbers that have an 8 in the tens place.

| 108 | 86 | 282 |
| 864 | 198 | 38 |

34 There are 30 students in a class. The teacher needs to divide the students in the class into teams. Each team must have the same number of students in it. There cannot be any students left over. Which of the following could describe the teams?

Ⓐ 7 teams of 4 students

Ⓑ 8 teams of 4 students

Ⓒ 6 teams of 5 students

Ⓓ 10 teams of 2 students

35 There were 16 people on a bus. At the first bus stop, 4 people got off the bus. Which expression can be used to find the number of people left on the bus?

Ⓐ   16 + 4

Ⓑ   16 ÷ 4

Ⓒ   16 − 4

Ⓓ   16 × 4

36 Look at the number pattern below. If the pattern continues, which number will come next? Write your answer on the blank line.

7, 10, 13, 16, 19, 22, ____

37 The pictograph below shows how many emails Sammy received each week day.

Monday	✉✉✉
Tuesday	✉✉
Wednesday	✉✉✉✉
Thursday	✉✉✉
Friday	✉✉✉✉✉✉

Each ✉ means 2 emails.

How many emails did Sammy receive on Wednesday?

Ⓐ 8

Ⓑ 6

Ⓒ 4

Ⓓ 3

38   What time is shown on the clock below?

Ⓐ   6:30

Ⓑ   7:30

Ⓒ   6:15

Ⓓ   6:45

39 Naomi is making a pictograph to show how many fruit trees there are in her yard. The pictograph she has made so far is shown below.

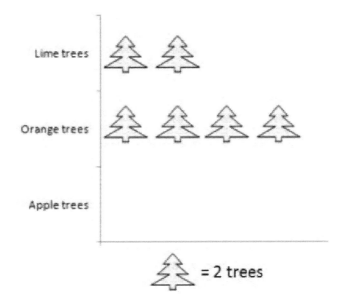

There are 6 apple trees in Naomi's yard. How many tree symbols should Naomi use to show 6 apple trees?

Ⓐ 3

Ⓑ 2

Ⓒ 12

Ⓓ 6

40 Lydia eats 2 pieces of fruit every day. Which table shows how many pieces of fruit Lydia eats in 5, 7, and 14 days?

Ⓐ

Number of Days	Number of Pieces of Fruit
5	10
7	14
14	18

Ⓑ

Number of Days	Number of Pieces of Fruit
5	10
7	14
14	20

Ⓒ

Number of Days	Number of Pieces of Fruit
5	10
7	15
14	30

Ⓓ

Number of Days	Number of Pieces of Fruit
5	10
7	14
14	28

41 A recipe for meatballs calls for $\frac{1}{2}$ teaspoon of cumin. Which fraction is equivalent to $\frac{1}{2}$?

Ⓐ $\frac{2}{6}$

Ⓑ $\frac{2}{4}$

Ⓒ $\frac{4}{6}$

Ⓓ $\frac{3}{2}$

42 The picture below represents a playground.

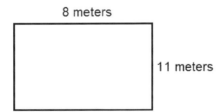

8 meters

11 meters

What is the perimeter of the playground?

Ⓐ   19 meters

Ⓑ   38 meters

Ⓒ   57 meters

Ⓓ   88 meters

43   Which of the following describes a rhombus?

    Ⓐ   6 edges

    Ⓑ   6 vertices

    Ⓒ   4 right angles

    Ⓓ   4 congruent sides

44   Which fraction model is equivalent to $\frac{1}{4}$?

    Ⓐ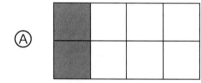

    Ⓑ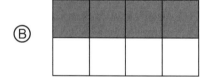

    Ⓒ

    Ⓓ

45   What part of the model is shaded?

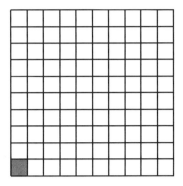

(A) $\dfrac{1}{10}$

(B) $\dfrac{10}{1}$

(C) $\dfrac{1}{100}$

(D) $\dfrac{100}{1}$

46   A school has 7 school buses. Each bus can seat 48 students. What is the total number of students the buses can seat?

(A)   266

(B)   336

(C)   288

(D)   284

47 What is the length of the piece of lace shown below?

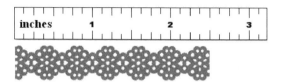

Ⓐ   2 inches

Ⓑ   2.5 inches

Ⓒ   1.5 inches

Ⓓ   2.2 inches

48 The graph below shows how far four students travel to school.

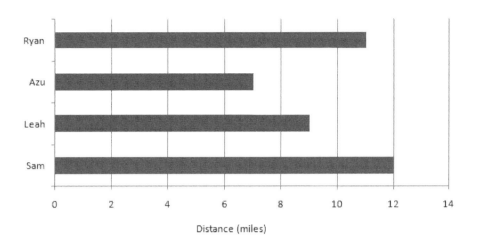

How much farther does Ryan travel than Azu?

Ⓐ 7 miles

Ⓑ 11 miles

Ⓒ 4 miles

Ⓓ 3 miles

49 Malcolm surveyed some people to find out how many pets they owned. The line plot shows the results of the survey.

Number of Pets

```
                    X
        X           X
        X           X
        X           X       X
        X           X       X       X       X
        X           X       X       X       X
    _____
        0           1       2       3       4
```

How many people owned 2 or more pets?

Ⓐ   3

Ⓑ   4

Ⓒ   7

Ⓓ   9

50 The picture below represents a floor rug.

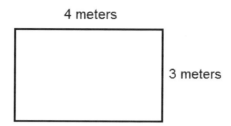

4 meters

3 meters

What is the perimeter of the floor rug?

Ⓐ 14 meters

Ⓑ 12 meters

Ⓒ 7 meters

Ⓓ 21 meters

END OF SECTION 2

SOL MATHEMATICS

GRADE 3

PRACTICE TEST 3

SECTION 1

Instructions

Read each question carefully. For each multiple-choice question, fill in the circle for the correct answer. For other types of questions, follow the instructions given.

1   A bookstore sold 40,905 books in May. Which of these is another way to write 40,905?

Ⓐ   Four thousand nine hundred and five

Ⓑ   Forty thousand ninety five

Ⓒ   Four thousand ninety five

Ⓓ   Forty thousand nine hundred and five

2   Which of the following shapes is a pentagon?

Ⓐ

Ⓑ

Ⓒ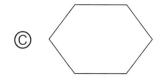

Ⓓ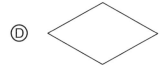

3   Which point on the number line represents 46?

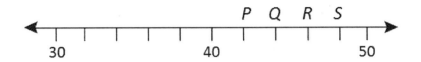

Ⓐ   Point *P*

Ⓑ   Point *Q*

Ⓒ   Point *R*

Ⓓ   Point *S*

4   Sam read 39 pages of a novel in one week. He had 165 pages left to read. How many pages does the novel have?

Ⓐ   204

Ⓑ   136

Ⓒ   194

Ⓓ   126

5 Which number has a 3 in the thousands place?

 Ⓐ 10,386

 Ⓑ 35,689

 © 23,782

 Ⓓ 71,935

6 Leonie has 20 books. She placed an equal number of books on 5 different shelves. There were no books left over.

Which number sentence shows how many books Leonie put on each shelf?

 Ⓐ 20 + 5 = 25

 Ⓑ 20 − 5 = 15

 © 20 × 5 = 100

 Ⓓ 20 ÷ 5 = 4

7 Which of the following has $\frac{1}{3}$ of the stars shaded?

Ⓐ

Ⓑ

Ⓒ

Ⓓ

8 Stevie had $1.45. She bought a drink for $1.20. Stevie was given one coin as change. Which coin should Stevie have been given?

Ⓐ A dime

Ⓑ A penny

Ⓒ A quarter

Ⓓ A nickel

9 Look at the shaded figure below.

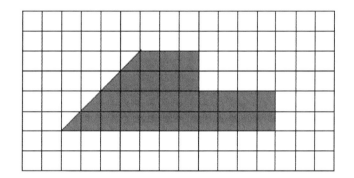

What is the area of the shaded figure?

Ⓐ 27 square units

Ⓑ 28 square units

Ⓒ 29 square units

Ⓓ 30 square units

10 Dannii is training for a bike race. She rode 17 miles on Monday, 19 miles on Tuesday, and 11 miles on Wednesday. Which is the best estimate of how far Dannii rode in all?

Ⓐ 30 miles

Ⓑ 40 miles

Ⓒ 50 miles

Ⓓ 60 miles

11 How many faces does the square pyramid shown below have?

Ⓐ 4

Ⓑ 5

Ⓒ 6

Ⓓ 8

12 Damon rode 3 miles to school every morning, and 3 miles back home each afternoon. How many miles would he ride in 5 days?

    Ⓐ   15 miles

    Ⓑ   30 miles

    Ⓒ   45 miles

    Ⓓ   60 miles

13 Which two shapes have the same number of sides?

    Ⓐ   Triangle and rectangle

    Ⓑ   Rectangle and square

    Ⓒ   Hexagon and pentagon

    Ⓓ   Pentagon and triangle

14   Look at the shapes below. Circle the two shapes that appear to be congruent.

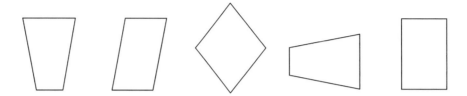

15   Which measurement best describes the length of a football field?

Ⓐ   360 feet

Ⓑ   360 inches

Ⓒ   360 centimeters

Ⓓ   360 kilometers

16 What are the two smallest numbers that can be made using the digits 1, 6, and 4? Each digit must be used only once in each number. Write your answer on the lines below.

_____ _____ _____

_____ _____ _____

17 The school library has 1,532 fiction books, 1,609 non-fiction books, and 1,239 children's books. Which number sentence shows the best way to estimate the total number of books?

Ⓐ   1,500 + 1,600 + 1,200 = 4,300

Ⓑ   1,500 + 1,600 + 1,300 = 4,400

Ⓒ   1,600 + 1,600 + 1,300 = 4,500

Ⓓ   1,600 + 1,700 + 1,300 = 4,600

18 Jennifer painted the eggs below for a craft project.

What fraction of the eggs are striped?

(A) $\frac{1}{2}$

(B) $\frac{1}{3}$

(C) $\frac{2}{3}$

(D) $\frac{2}{5}$

19 The thermometer below shows the temperature at 5 p.m. on Tuesday.

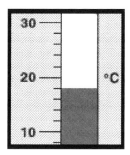

By 10 p.m. on Tuesday, the temperature had dropped by 4°C. Show the temperate at 10 p.m. on Tuesday on the thermometer below.

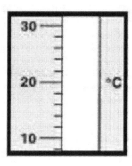

20 Which point on the number line represents $3\frac{1}{4}$?

Ⓐ   Point *F*

Ⓑ   Point *G*

Ⓒ   Point *H*

Ⓓ   Point *J*

21 A company has 28 salespersons. Each salesperson works about 37 hours each week. About how many hours do all the salespeople work in all?

Ⓐ   70

Ⓑ   600

Ⓒ   900

Ⓓ   1,200

22 A box contains 24 cans of soups. Gerald orders 8 boxes of soup for his store. He is charged $0.50 for each can of soup. What is the total cost of the soup Gerald ordered?

Ⓐ $12

Ⓑ $64

Ⓒ $96

Ⓓ $384

23 Which shape has exactly 6 sides?

Ⓐ   Triangle

Ⓑ   Pentagon

Ⓒ   Octagon

Ⓓ   Hexagon

24 Which measurement is the most likely weight of the apple shown below?

   Ⓐ   6 pounds

   Ⓑ   6 ounces

   Ⓒ   6 grams

   Ⓓ   6 kilograms

25 What is the perimeter of the rectangle below?

3 cm

10 cm

   Ⓐ   13 cm

   Ⓑ   30 cm

   Ⓒ   26 cm

   Ⓓ   60 cm

END OF SECTION 1

SOL MATHEMATICS

GRADE 3

PRACTICE TEST 3

SECTION 2

Instructions

Read each question carefully. For each multiple-choice question, fill in the circle for the correct answer. For other types of questions, follow the instructions given.

26 Which number sentence represents the array shown below?

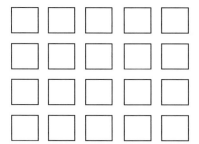

(A) $5 + 4 = 9$

(B) $5 \times 5 = 25$

(C) $5 \times 4 = 20$

(D) $5 - 4 = 1$

27 Tomato plants were planted in rows. Each row had the same number of tomato plants.

Number of Rows	Number of Tomato Plants
3	24
4	32
5	40
6	48

Based on the table above, how many tomato plants were in each row?

Ⓐ   24

Ⓑ   8

Ⓒ   6

Ⓓ   10

28 Rima found the money shown below while cleaning her father's car. How much money did Rima find?

Ⓐ $1.37

Ⓑ $1.62

Ⓒ $1.67

Ⓓ $1.92

29 Melinda buys bagels in packets of 4.

If Melinda counts the bagels in groups of 4, which number could she count?

Ⓐ   12

Ⓑ   10

Ⓒ   15

Ⓓ   18

30 Tim scored 21 points in a basketball game. Emmett scored 7 more points than Tim. Which method can be used to find how many points Tim and Emmett scored together?

Ⓐ   Add 21 and 7

Ⓑ   Add 21 to the sum of 21 and 7

Ⓒ   Add 21 to the difference of 21 and 7

Ⓓ   Subtract 7 from 21

31 Which number is less than $\frac{5}{12}$?

    Ⓐ $\frac{1}{2}$

    Ⓑ $\frac{1}{3}$

    Ⓒ $\frac{5}{6}$

    Ⓓ $\frac{7}{12}$

32 Mrs. Anderson took out a loan that will take her 60 months to pay off. How many years will it take Mrs. Anderson to pay off the loan? Write your answer on the line below.

_____ years

33 Place the names of the shapes below in order from the least sides to the most sides.

square   triangle   hexagon   pentagon

Least   _____

               _____

               _____

Most   _____

34 There are 28 students at basketball training. The coach needs to divide the students into groups. Each group must have the same number of students in it. There cannot be any students left over. Which of the following could describe the groups?

Ⓐ   7 groups of 4 students

Ⓑ   8 groups of 3 students

Ⓒ   6 groups of 4 students

Ⓓ   10 groups of 3 students

35 Annie collects baseball cards. She has 22 cards in her collection. She gave her sister 2 baseball cards. Then Annie bought 4 new baseball cards. Which expression can be used to find the number of baseball cards Annie has now?

Ⓐ   22 + 2 + 4

Ⓑ   22 + 2 − 4

Ⓒ   22 − 2 + 4

Ⓓ   22 − 2 − 4

36 Nate created the pattern below.

If Nate continues the pattern, how many circles would there be in the next step of the pattern?

Ⓐ   12

Ⓑ   14

Ⓒ   15

Ⓓ   25

37   The pictograph below shows how long Tamika spent at the computer each week day.

Monday	🖥 🖥 🖥 🖥
Tuesday	🖥 🖥 🖥 🖥 🖥 🖥
Wednesday	🖥 🖥 🖥 🖥 🖥
Thursday	🖥 🖥 🖥
Friday	🖥 🖥

Each 🖥 means 10 minutes.

How long did Tamika spend at the computer on Wednesday?

Ⓐ   15 minutes

Ⓑ   60 minutes

Ⓒ   5 minutes

Ⓓ   50 minutes

38 What time is shown on the clock below?

Ⓐ 12:30

Ⓑ 12:00

Ⓒ 6:00

Ⓓ 6:30

39 Ming is making a pictograph to show how many boys are in grade 3, grade 4, and grade 5. The pictograph she has made so far is shown below.

Grade 3	☺☺☺☺☺☺
Grade 4	☺☺☺☺☺☺☺
Grade 5	

Each ☺ means 5 boys.

There are 50 boys in grade 5. Which of the following shows what Ming should put in the grade 5 row of the pictograph?

Ⓐ   ☺☺☺☺☺

Ⓑ   ☺☺☺☺☺☺☺

Ⓒ   ☺☺☺☺☺☺☺☺☺

Ⓓ   ☺☺☺☺☺☺☺☺☺☺

40 Lei jogs for 15 minutes every day. Which table shows how long Lei jogs for in 4, 5, and 6 days?

Ⓐ

Number of Days	Number of Minutes Jogged
4	60
5	65
6	70

Ⓑ

Number of Days	Number of Minutes Jogged
4	60
5	90
6	120

Ⓒ

Number of Days	Number of Minutes Jogged
4	15
5	30
6	45

Ⓓ

Number of Days	Number of Minutes Jogged
4	60
5	75
6	90

41 Dean drew these shapes.

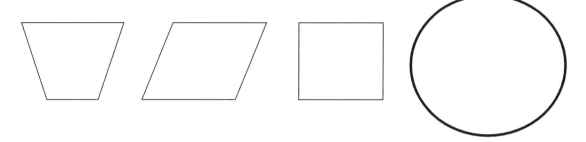

Selma drew these shapes.

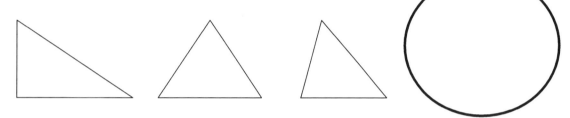

Add one of the shapes below to Dean's shapes and one of the shapes below to Selma's shapes. Draw each shape in the empty circle.

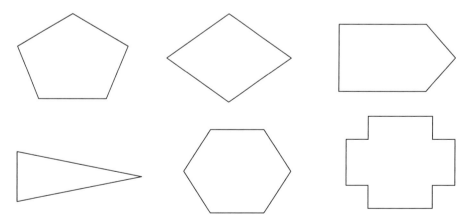

42 Which of the following shows the shape of the base of the square pyramid below?

Ⓐ

Ⓑ

Ⓒ

Ⓓ

43 During the baseball season, Marvin's team won 5 games and lost 14 games.

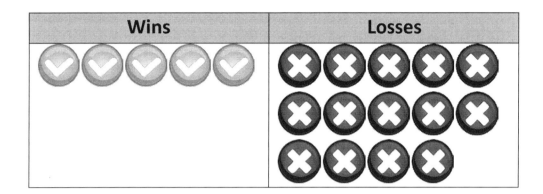

What fraction of its total games did the team win?

Ⓐ $\dfrac{5}{14}$

Ⓑ $\dfrac{14}{19}$

Ⓒ $\dfrac{5}{19}$

Ⓓ $\dfrac{5}{9}$

44   On the diagram below, what does the circled area of the diagram show?

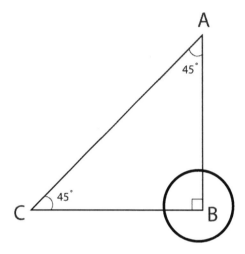

Ⓐ   A ray

Ⓑ   An angle

Ⓒ   A line segment

Ⓓ   A point

45   A piece of note paper has side lengths of 5 inches. What is the perimeter of the note paper?

Ⓐ   10 inches

Ⓑ   20 inches

Ⓒ   25 inches

Ⓓ   30 inches

46 Rita made the pictograph below to show how many cans each class collected for a food drive.

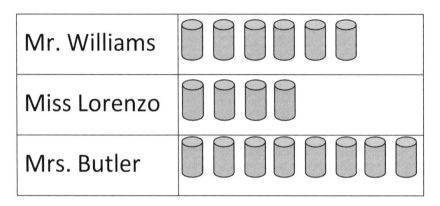

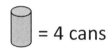 = 4 cans

How many cans did Miss Lorenzo's class collect?

Ⓐ 4

Ⓑ 8

Ⓒ 16

Ⓓ 24

47 Which number makes the number sentence below true? Write the number in the box.

$$9 + \boxed{} = 7 + 9$$

48 Kim is 63 inches tall. Chelsea is 4 inches taller than Kim. Vicky is 3 inches shorter than Chelsea. Which expression could be used to find Vicky's height, in inches?

Ⓐ $63 - 4 - 3$

Ⓑ $63 + 4 + 3$

Ⓒ $63 - 4 + 3$

Ⓓ $63 + 4 - 3$

49   What is the perimeter of the triangle shown below?

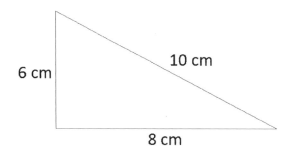

(A)   12 cm

(B)   22 cm

(C)   24 cm

(D)   48 cm

50   Kym is going camping. It costs $16 per night for the campsite. Kym plans to stay for 8 nights. How much will the campsite cost for 8 nights?

(A) $128

(B) $132

(C) $148

(D) $152

END OF SECTION 2

ANSWER KEY

Tracking Student Progress

Use the answer key to score each practice test. After scoring each test, record the score in the Score Tracker at the back of the book.

As the student progresses, test scores will continue to improve as the student gains experience, knowledge, and confidence.

Topics and Math Skills

The SOL Mathematics test given by the state tests a specific set of skills and knowledge. The state divides these skills into six broad areas, or topics. These are:

- Number & Number Sense
- Computation & Estimation
- Measurement
- Geometry
- Probability & Statistics
- Patterns, Functions, and Algebra

The answer key identifies the topic for each question. Use the topics listed to identify general areas of strength and weakness. Then target revision and instruction accordingly.

The answer key also identifies the specific math skill that each question is testing. Use the skills listed to identify skills that the student is lacking. Then target revision and instruction accordingly.

PRACTICE TEST 1 ANSWER KEY

Question	Answer	Topic	Math Skill
1	A	Number & Number Sense	Use place value to understand numbers
2	Bar to 9 Bar to 5	Probability & Statistics	Construct a bar graph to represent data
3	A	Number & Number Sense	Compare fractions using models
4	D	Computation & Estimation	Understand and solve multistep problems
5	C	Number & Number Sense	Identify place value
6	C	Computation & Estimation	Use division to solve problems
7	Any 5 stars shaded	Number & Number Sense	Model fractions
8	A	Computation & Estimation	Understand and solve multistep problems
9	A	Measurement	Determine area by counting squares
10	C	Computation & Estimation	Use estimation to solve problems
11		Geometry	Identify and compare plane figures
12	C	Number & Number Sense	Use the multiplication/division relationship
13	1	Patterns, Functions, Algebra	Understand the identity property of multiplication
14	A	Geometry	Identify congruent shapes
15	D	Measurement	Estimate measurements of length
16	9,851	Number & Number Sense	Use place value to solve problems
17	B	Number & Number Sense	Use rounding to make estimates
18	B	Number & Number Sense	Write fractions represented by a model
19	C	Computation & Estimation	Represent multiplication using models
20	D	Number & Number Sense	Represent fractions on a number line
21	B	Probability & Statistics	Understand and apply probability as chance
22	A	Computation & Estimation	Use multiplication to solve problems
23	C	Geometry	Compare and contrast plane figures
24	C	Measurement	Estimate measurements of perimeter
25	B	Geometry	Identify solid figures

Question	Answer	Topic	Math Skill
26	C	Measurement	Determine the value of a collection of coins
27	C	Patterns, Functions, Algebra	Recognize and describe patterns
28	B	Measurement	Determine the value of a collection of coins
29	18, 30, 36	Patterns, Functions, Algebra	Recognize and describe patterns
30	A	Computation & Estimation	Solve problems that involve multiplication
31	D	Computation & Estimation	Understand and solve multistep problems
32	C	Probability & Statistics	Read and interpret bar graphs
33	C	Number & Number Sense	Compare fractions using models
34	D	Computation & Estimation	Solve problems that involve multiplication
35	D	Computation & Estimation	Understand and solve multistep problems
36	B	Patterns, Functions, Algebra	Extend number patterns
37	A	Probability & Statistics	Read and interpret bar graphs
38	B	Measurement	Tell time using clocks
39	B	Probability & Statistics	Construct a picture graph to represent data
40	A	Patterns, Functions, Algebra	Recognize and describe patterns
41	B	Probability & Statistics	Read and interpret bar graphs
42	6, 6	Geometry	Describe the characteristics of plane figures
43	C	Geometry	Identify solid figures
44	A	Number & Number Sense	Write fractions represented by a model
45	B	Measurement	Determine elapsed time
46	C	Probability & Statistics	Collect and organize data
47	A	Number & Number Sense	Compare fractions using models
48	B	Probability & Statistics	Construct a picture graph to represent data
49	B	Measurement	Identify equivalent periods of time
50	D	Number & Number Sense	Write fractions represented by a model

PRACTICE TEST 2
ANSWER KEY

Question	Answer	Topic	Math Skill
1	A	Number & Number Sense	Use place value to understand numbers
2	C	Probability & Statistics	Read and interpret bar graphs
3	Point at 48	Number & Number Sense	Represent numbers on a number line
4	B	Computation & Estimation	Use addition and subtraction to solve problems
5	A	Number & Number Sense	Identify place value
6	B	Computation & Estimation	Use division to solve problems
7	D	Number & Number Sense	Model fractions
8	C	Computation & Estimation	Understand and solve multistep problems
9	A	Measurement	Determine area by counting squares
10	C	Computation & Estimation	Use estimation to solve problems
11	C	Probability & Statistics	Understand and apply probability as chance
12	B	Computation & Estimation	Understand and solve multistep problems
13	B	Geometry	Compare and contrast plane figures
14	1st, 3rd, and 4th triangle circled	Geometry	Identify congruent shapes
15	B	Measurement	Estimate measurements of length
16	A	Number & Number Sense	Use rounding to make estimates
17	A	Computation & Estimation	Use addition and subtraction to solve problems
18	D	Number & Number Sense	Write fractions represented by a model
19	D	Probability & Statistics	Understand and apply probability as chance
20	A	Number & Number Sense	Write fractions represented by a model
21	cone, cylinder	Geometry	Identify solid figures
22	B	Computation & Estimation	Use multiplication to solve problems
23	A	Number & Number Sense	Use the multiplication/division relationship
24	B	Measurement	Estimate measurements of length
25	D	Measurement	Determine the perimeter of a polygon

Question	Answer	Topic	Math Skill
26	A	Patterns, Functions, Algebra	Recognize and describe patterns
27	C	Patterns, Functions, Algebra	Identify and extend patterns
28	A	Measurement	Determine the value of a collection of coins
29	C	Patterns, Functions, Algebra	Recognize and describe patterns
30	49 < 51 < 57	Number & Number Sense	Compare and order numbers
31	B	Number & Number Sense	Compare and order numbers
32	Bar to 16 Bar to 14 Bar to 18	Probability & Statistics	Construct a bar graph to represent data
33	86, 282	Number & Number Sense	Identify place value
34	C	Computation & Estimation	Use multiplication to solve problems
35	C	Computation & Estimation	Use subtraction to solve problems
36	25	Patterns, Functions, Algebra	Extend number patterns
37	A	Probability & Statistics	Read and interpret picture graphs
38	B	Measurement	Tell time using clocks
39	A	Probability & Statistics	Construct a picture graph to represent data
40	D	Patterns, Functions, Algebra	Recognize and describe patterns
41	B	Number & Number Sense	Compare fractions
42	B	Measurement	Determine the perimeter of a polygon
43	D	Geometry	Identify and describe plane figures
44	A	Number & Number Sense	Compare fractions using models
45	C	Number & Number Sense	Write fractions represented by a model
46	B	Computation & Estimation	Use multiplication to solve problems
47	B	Measurement	Measure length
48	C	Probability & Statistics	Read and interpret bar graphs
49	C	Probability & Statistics	Read and interpret line plots
50	A	Measurement	Determine the perimeter of a polygon

PRACTICE TEST 3 ANSWER KEY

Question	Answer	Topic	Math Skill
1	D	Number & Number Sense	Read and write numerals
2	A	Geometry	Identify polygons
3	C	Number & Number Sense	Represent numbers on a number line
4	A	Computation & Estimation	Use addition and subtraction to solve problems
5	C	Number & Number Sense	Identify place value
6	D	Computation & Estimation	Represent division using models
7	D	Number & Number Sense	Model fractions
8	C	Measurement	Compare the value of coins and make change
9	B	Measurement	Determine area by counting squares
10	C	Computation & Estimation	Use estimation to solve problems
11	B	Geometry	Describe the characteristics of solid figures
12	B	Computation & Estimation	Understand and solve multistep problems
13	B	Geometry	Compare and contrast plane figures
14	1st and 4th circled	Geometry	Identify congruent shapes
15	A	Measurement	Estimate measurements of length
16	146, 164	Number & Number Sense	Use place value to solve problems
17	A	Number & Number Sense	Use rounding to make estimates
18	D	Number & Number Sense	Write fractions represented by a model
19	14°C	Measurement	Use thermometers to measure temperature
20	B	Number & Number Sense	Represent fractions on a number line
21	D	Computation & Estimation	Use estimation to solve problems
22	C	Computation & Estimation	Understand and solve multistep problems
23	D	Geometry	Identify and describe plane figures
24	B	Measurement	Estimate measurements of weight/mass
25	C	Measurement	Determine the perimeter of a polygon

Question	Answer	Topic	Math Skill
26	C	Computation & Estimation	Represent multiplication using models
27	B	Patterns, Functions, Algebra	Recognize and describe patterns
28	C	Measurement	Determine the value of a collection of bills/coins
29	A	Patterns, Functions, Algebra	Recognize and describe patterns
30	B	Computation & Estimation	Understand and solve multistep problems
31	B	Number & Number Sense	Compare fractions
32	5 years	Measurement	Identify equivalent periods of time
33	triangle square pentagon hexagon	Geometry	Compare and contrast plane figures
34	A	Computation & Estimation	Solve problems that involve multiplication
35	C	Computation & Estimation	Use addition and subtraction to solve problems
36	C	Patterns, Functions, Algebra	Identify and extend patterns
37	D	Probability & Statistics	Read and interpret picture graphs
38	C	Measurement	Tell time using clocks
39	C	Probability & Statistics	Construct a picture graph to represent data
40	D	Patterns, Functions, Algebra	Recognize and describe patterns
41	Dean: kite Selma: triangle	Geometry	Compare and contrast plane figures
42	D	Geometry	Describe the characteristics of solid figures
43	C	Number & Number Sense	Write fractions represented by a model
44	B	Geometry	Identify points, line segments, rays, and angles
45	B	Measurement	Determine the perimeter of a polygon
46	C	Probability & Statistics	Read and interpret picture graphs
47	7	Patterns, Functions, Algebra	Understand the commutative property
48	D	Computation & Estimation	Use addition and subtraction to solve problems
49	C	Measurement	Determine the perimeter of a polygon
50	A	Computation & Estimation	Use multiplication to solve problems

SCORE TRACKER

Test	Score
Practice Test 1	/50
Practice Test 2	/50
Practice Test 3	/50

VIRGINIA READING TEST PREP

For reading test prep, get the Virginia Test Prep Practice Test Book. It contains 6 reading mini-tests, focused vocabulary quizzes, plus a full-length SOL Reading practice test.

48218426R00066

Made in the USA
Middletown, DE
13 September 2017